THE SECRET GARDEN

"We're alike, you and me," old Ben Weatherstaff said to Mary. "We're not pretty to look at, and we're both very disagreeable."

angry.

Poor Mary! Nobody wants her, and nobody likes her. Her parents have died, and she is sent home from India to live in her uncle's house in Yorkshire. It is a big old house, with nearly a hundred rooms, but most of them are shut and locked. Mary is cross, bored, and lonely. There is nothing to do all day, and no one to talk to, except old Ben Weatherstaff, the gardener.

But then Mary learns about the secret garden. The door is locked and hidden, and the key is lost. No one has been inside the secret garden for ten years—except the robin, who flies over the wall. Mary watches the robin, and wonders where the key is …

And then there is that strange crying in the night, somewhere in the house. It sounds like a child crying …

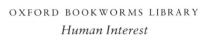

OXFORD BOOKWORMS LIBRARY

Human Interest

The Secret Garden

Stage 3 (1000 headwords)

Series Editor: Jennifer Bassett
Founder Editor: Tricia Hedge
Activities Editors: Jennifer Bassett and Alison Baxter

American Edition: Daphne Mackey, University of Washington

FRANCES HODGSON BURNETT

The
Secret Garden

Retold by
Clare West

Illustrated by
Jenny Brackley

OXFORD UNIVERSITY PRESS

OXFORD

UNIVERSITY PRESS

Great Clarendon Street, Oxford OX2 6DP

Oxford University Press is a department of the University of Oxford.
It furthers the University's objective of excellence in research, scholarship,
and education by publishing worldwide in

Oxford New York

Auckland Cape Town Dar es Salaam Hong Kong Karachi
Kuala Lumpur Madrid Melbourne Mexico City Nairobi
New Delhi Shanghai Taipei Toronto

With offices in

Argentina Austria Brazil Chile Czech Republic France Greece
Guatemala Hungary Italy Japan Poland Portugal Singapore
South Korea Switzerland Thailand Turkey Ukraine Vietnam

OXFORD and OXFORD ENGLISH are registered trade marks of
Oxford University Press in the UK and in certain other countries

This edition © Oxford University Press 2007

Database right Oxford University Press (maker)

First published in Oxford Bookworms 1993

10

ISBN 978 0 19 423754 3

Typeset by Wyvern Typesetting Ltd. Bristol

Printed in China

CONTENTS

1910 y

1
Little Miss Mary

Nobody seemed to care about Mary. She was born in India, where her father was a British official. He was busy with his work, and her mother, who was very beautiful, spent all her time going to parties. So an Indian woman, Kamala, was paid to take care of the little girl. Mary was not a pretty child. She had a thin angry face and thin yellow hair. She was always giving orders to Kamala, who had to obey. Mary never thought of other people, but only of herself. In fact, she was a very selfish, disagreeable, bad-tempered little girl.

One very hot morning, when she was about nine years old, she woke up and saw that instead of Kamala there was a different Indian servant by her bed.

Mary saw that there was a different Indian servant by her bed.

"What are *you* doing here?" she asked crossly. "Go away! And send Kamala to me at once!"

The woman looked afraid. "I'm sorry, Miss Mary, she—she—she can't come!"

Something strange was happening that day. Some of the house servants were missing, and everybody looked frightened. But nobody told Mary anything, and Kamala still did not come. So at last Mary went out into the garden and played by herself under a tree. She pretended she was making her own flower garden, and she picked large red flowers to push into the ground. All the time she was saying crossly to herself,

"I hate Kamala! I'll hit her when she comes back!"

Just then she saw her mother coming into the garden, with a young Englishman. They did not notice the child, who listened to their conversation.

"It's very bad, is it?" her mother asked the young man in a worried voice.

"Very bad," he answered seriously. "People are dying like flies. It's dangerous to stay in this town. You should go to the hills, where there's no disease."

"Oh, I know!" she cried. "We need to leave soon!"

Suddenly they heard loud cries coming from the servants' rooms at the side of the house.

"What's happened?" cried Mary's mother wildly.

"I think one of your servants has just died. You didn't tell me the disease is *here*, in your house!"

"I didn't know!" she screamed. "Quick, come with me!"

2

"You didn't tell me the disease is here, *in your house!"*

And together they ran into the house.

Now Mary understood what was wrong. The terrible disease had already killed many people in the town, and in all the houses people were dying. In Mary's house it was Kamala who had just died. Later that day three more servants died there.

3

All through the night and the next day people ran in and out of the house, shouting and crying. Nobody thought of Mary. She hid in her bedroom, frightened by the strange and terrible sounds that she heard around her. Sometimes she cried, and sometimes she slept.

When she woke up the next day, the house was silent.

"Perhaps the disease has gone," she thought, "and everybody is well again. I wonder who will take care of me instead of Kamala? Why doesn't someone bring me some food? It's strange the house is so quiet."

But just then she heard men's voices in the hall.

"How sad!" said one. "That beautiful woman!"

"There was a child too, wasn't there?" said the other. "Although none of us ever saw her."

Mary was standing in the middle of her room when they opened the door a few minutes later. The two men jumped back in surprise.

"My name is Mary Lennox," she said crossly. "I was asleep when everyone was ill, and now I'm hungry."

"It's the child, the one nobody ever saw!" said the older man to the other. "They've all forgotten her!"

"*Why* was I forgotten?" asked Mary angrily. "*Why* has nobody come to take care of me?"

The younger man looked at her very sadly. "Poor child!" he said. "You see, there's nobody left alive in the house. So nobody *can* come."

In this strange and sudden way Mary learned that both her mother and her father had died. The few servants who had not died had run away in the night. No one had remembered little Miss Mary. She was all alone.

Because she had never known her parents well, she did not miss them at all. She only thought of herself, as she had always done.

"Where will I live?" she wondered. "I hope I'll stay with people who'll let me do what I want."

At first she was taken to an English family who had known her parents. She hated their untidy house and noisy children, and preferred playing by herself in the garden. One day she was playing her favorite game, pretending to make a garden, when one of the children, Basil, offered to help.

"Go away!" cried Mary. "I don't want your help!"

For a moment Basil looked angry, and then he began to laugh. He danced around and around Mary and sang a funny little song about Miss Mary and her stupid flowers. This made Mary very angry. No one had ever laughed at her so unkindly.

"You're going home soon," said Basil. "And we're all very happy you're leaving!"

"I'm happy too," replied Mary. "But where's home?"

"You're stupid if you don't know that!" laughed Basil. "England, of course! You're going to live with your uncle, Mr. Archibald Craven."

"I've never heard of him," said Mary coldly.

"But *I* know about him because I heard Father and Mother talking," said Basil. "He lives in a big lonely old house, and he has no friends because he's so bad-tempered. He has a crooked back, and he's horrid!"

"I don't believe you!" cried Mary. But the next day Basil's parents explained that she was going to live with her uncle in Yorkshire, in the north of England. Mary looked bored and cross and said nothing.

"He has a crooked back, and he's horrid!"

After the long sea journey, she was met in London by Mr. Craven's housekeeper, Mrs. Medlock. Together they traveled north by train. Mrs. Medlock was a large woman, with a very red face and bright black eyes. Mary did not like her, but that was not surprising because she did not usually like people. Mrs. Medlock did not like Mary either.

"What a disagreeable child!" thought the housekeeper. "But perhaps I should talk to her."

"I can tell you a bit about your uncle if you like," she said aloud. "He lives in a big old house, a long way from anywhere. There are nearly a hundred rooms, but most of them are shut and locked. There's a big park around the house and all kinds of gardens. Well, what do you think of that?"

"Nothing," replied Mary. "It doesn't matter to me."

Mrs. Medlock laughed. "You're a hard little girl! Well, if *you* don't care, Mr. Craven doesn't either. He never spends time on anyone. He has a crooked back, you see, and although he's always been rich, he was never really happy until he married."

"Married?" repeated Mary in surprise.

"Yes, he married a sweet, pretty girl, and he loved her deeply. So when she died—"

"Oh! Did she die?" asked Mary, interested.

"Yes, she did. And now he doesn't care about anybody. If he's at home, he stays in his room and sees nobody. He won't want to see *you*, so you have to stay out of his way and do what you're told."

Mary stared out of the train window at the gray sky and the rain. She was not looking forward to life at her uncle's house.

The train journey lasted all day, and it was dark when they arrived at the station. Then there was a long drive to get to the house. It was a cold, windy night, and it was raining heavily. After a while Mary began to hear a strange, wild noise. She looked out of the window, but could see nothing except the darkness.

7

"What's that noise?" she asked Mrs. Medlock. "It's—It's not the sea, is it?"

"No, that's the moor. It's the sound the wind makes, blowing across the moor."

"It's the sound the wind makes, blowing across the moor."

"What is a moor?"

"It's just miles and miles of wild land, with no trees or houses. Your uncle's house is right on the edge of the moor."

Mary listened to the strange, frightening sound. "I don't like it," she thought. "I don't like it." She looked more disagreeable than ever.

2

Mary in Yorkshire

They arrived at a very large old house. It looked dark and unfriendly from the outside. Inside, Mary looked around the big shadowy hall and felt very small and lost. They went straight upstairs. Mary was shown to a room where there was a warm fire and food on the table.

"This is your room," said Mrs. Medlock. "Go to bed when you've had some supper. And remember, you have to stay in your room! Mr. Craven doesn't want you to wander all over the house!"

When Mary woke up the next morning, she saw a young servant girl cleaning the fireplace. The room seemed dark and rather strange, with pictures of dogs, horses, and ladies on the walls. It was not a child's room at all. From the window she could not see any trees or houses, only wild land, which looked like a kind of purple sea.

moor — bag spaci

"Who are you?" she asked the servant coldly.

"Martha, miss," answered the girl with a smile.

"And what's that outside?" Mary continued.

"That's the moor," smiled Martha. "Do you like it?"

"No," replied Mary immediately. "I hate it."

"That's because you don't know it. You *will* like it. I love it. It's wonderful in spring and summer when there are flowers. It always smells so sweet. The air's so fresh, and the birds sing so beautifully. I never want to leave the moor."

Mary was feeling very bad-tempered. "You're a strange servant," she said. "In India we don't have conversations with servants. We give orders, and they obey, and that's that."

Martha did not seem to mind Mary's crossness.

"I know I talk too much!" she laughed.

"Are you going to be *my* servant?" asked Mary.

"Well, not really. I work for Mrs. Medlock. I'm going to clean your room and bring you your food, but you won't need a servant except for those things."

"But who's going to dress me?"

Martha stopped cleaning and stared at Mary.

P 59 → "Tha' canna' dress thysen?" she asked, shocked.

"What do you mean? I don't understand your language!"

"Oh, I forgot. We all speak the Yorkshire dialect here, but of course you don't understand that. I meant to say, can't you put on your own clothes?"

"Of course not! My servant always used to dress me."

"Well! I think you should learn to dress yourself. My mother always says people should be able to take care of

10

extremely angry

themselves, even if they're rich and important."

Little Miss Mary was furious with Martha. "It's different in India where I come from! You don't know anything about India, or about servants, or about anything! You ... you ..." She could not explain what she meant. Suddenly she felt very confused and lonely. She threw herself down on the bed and started crying wildly.

Martha stopped cleaning and stared at Mary.

"Now, now, don't cry like that," Martha said gently. "I'm very sorry. You're right, I don't know anything about anything. Please stop crying, miss."

She sounded kind and friendly, and Mary began to feel better and soon stopped crying. Martha went on talking as she finished her cleaning, but Mary looked out of the window in a bored way and pretended not to listen.

"I have eleven brothers and sisters, you know, miss. There's not much money in our house. And they all eat so much food! Mother says it's the good fresh air on the moor that makes them so hungry. My brother Dickon, he's always out on the moor. He's twelve, and he has a horse which he rides sometimes."

"Where did he get it?" asked Mary. She had always wanted an animal of her own, and so she began to feel a little interest in Dickon.

"Oh, it's a wild horse, but he's a kind boy, and animals like him, you see. Now you need to have your breakfast, miss. Here it is on the table."

"I don't want it," said Mary. "I'm not hungry."

"What!" cried Martha. "My little brothers and sisters would eat all this in five minutes!"

"Why?" asked Mary coldly.

"Because they don't get enough to eat, that's why, and they're always hungry. You're very lucky to have the food, miss." Mary said nothing, but she drank some tea and ate a little bread.

"Now put a coat on and run outside to play," said

"I don't want it," said Mary. "I'm not hungry."

Martha. "It'll do you good to be in the fresh air."

Mary looked out of the window at the cold gray sky. "Why should I go out on a day like this?" she asked.

"Well, there's nothing to play with indoors, is there?"

Mary realized Martha was right. "But who will go with me?" she said.

Martha stared at her. "Nobody. You'll have to learn to play by yourself. Dickon plays by himself on the moors for hours, with the wild birds, the sheep, and the other animals." She looked away for a moment. "Perhaps I shouldn't tell you this, but—but one of the walled gardens is locked up. Nobody's been in it for ten years. It was Mrs. Craven's garden, and when she died so suddenly, Mr. Craven locked it and buried the key—Oh, I have to go, I can hear Mrs. Medlock's bell ringing for me."

Mary went downstairs and wandered through the great empty gardens. Many of the fruit and vegetable gardens had walls around them, but there were no locked doors. She saw an old man digging in one of the vegetable gardens, but he looked cross and unfriendly, so she walked on.

"How ugly it all looks in winter!" she thought. "But what a mystery the locked garden is! Why did my uncle bury the key? If he loved his wife, why did he hate her garden? Perhaps I'll never know. I don't suppose I'll like him if I ever meet him. And he won't like me, so I won't be able to ask him."

Just then she noticed a robin singing to her from a tree on the other side of a wall. "I think that tree's in the secret garden!" she told herself. "There's an extra wall here, and there's no way in."

She went back to where the gardener was digging and spoke to him. At first he answered in a very bad-tempered

Just then she noticed a robin.

way, but suddenly the robin flew down near them, and the old man began to smile. He looked a different person then, and Mary thought how much nicer people looked when they smiled. The gardener spoke gently to the robin, and the

14

pretty little bird hopped on the ground near them.

"He's my friend, he is," said the old man. "There aren't any other robins in the garden, so he's a bit lonely." He spoke in strong Yorkshire dialect, so Mary had to listen carefully to understand him.

She looked very hard at the robin. "I'm lonely too," she said. She had not realized this before.

"What's your name?" she asked the gardener.

"Ben Weatherstaff. I'm lonely myself. The robin's my only friend, you see."

"I don't have any friends at all," said Mary.

Yorkshire people always say what they are thinking, and old Ben was a Yorkshire moor man. "We're alike, you and me," he told Mary. "We're not pretty to look at, and we're both very disagreeable."

Nobody had ever said this to Mary before. "Am I really as ugly and disagreeable as Ben?" she wondered.

Suddenly the robin flew to a tree near Mary and started singing to her. Ben laughed loudly.

"Well!" he said. "He wants to be your friend!"

"Oh! Would you please be my friend?" she whispered to the robin. She spoke in a soft, quiet voice, and old Ben looked at her in surprise.

"You said that really nicely!" he said. "You sound like Dickon, when he talks to animals on the moor."

"Do you know Dickon?" asked Mary. But just then the robin flew away. "Oh look, he's flown into the garden with no door! Please, Ben, how can I get into it?"

Ben stopped smiling and picked up his spade. "You can't, and that's that. It's not your business. Nobody can find the door. Run away and play, will you? I need to get on with my work." And he walked away. He did not even say goodbye.

Ben stopped smiling and picked up his spade.

In the next few days Mary spent almost all her time in the gardens. The fresh air from the moor made her hungry, and she was becoming stronger and healthier. One day she noticed the robin again. He was on top of a wall, singing to her. "Good morning! Isn't this fun! Come this way!" he seemed to say, as he hopped along the wall. Mary began to laugh as she danced along beside him. "I know the secret garden's on the other side of this wall!" she thought excitedly. "And the robin lives there! But where's the door?"

That evening she asked Martha to stay and talk to her beside the fire after supper. They could hear the wind blowing around the old house, but the room was warm and comfortable. Mary only had one idea in her head.

"Tell me about the secret garden," she said.

"Well, all right then, miss, but we aren't supposed to talk about it, you know. It was Mrs. Craven's favorite garden, and she and Mr. Craven used to take care of it themselves. They spent hours there, reading and talking. Very happy, they were. They used the branch of an old tree as a seat. But one day when she was sitting on the branch, it broke, and she fell. She was very badly hurt, and the next day she died. That's why he hates the garden so much and won't let anyone go in there."

"How sad!" said Mary. "Poor Mr. Craven!" It was the first time that she had ever felt sorry for anyone.

Just then, as she was listening to the wind outside, she heard another noise, in the house.

"Can you hear a child crying?" she asked Martha.

Martha looked confused. "Er—no," she replied. "No, I think … it must be the wind."

But at that moment the wind blew open their door, and they heard the crying very clearly.

"I told you!" cried Mary.

At once Martha shut the door. "It was the wind," she repeated. But she did not speak in her usual natural way, and Mary did not believe her.

The next day it was very rainy, so Mary did not go out. Instead she decided to wander around the house, looking into some of the hundred rooms that Mrs. Medlock had told her about. She spent all morning going in and out of dark, silent rooms, which were full of heavy furniture and old pictures. She saw no servants at all and was on her way back to her room for lunch, when she heard a cry. "It's a bit like the cry that I heard last night!" she thought. Just then the house-keeper, Mrs. Medlock, appeared, with her keys in her hand.

Just then Mrs. Medlock appeared.

"What are you doing here?" she asked crossly.

"I didn't know which way to go, and I heard someone crying," answered Mary.

"You didn't hear anything! Go back to your room now. And if you don't stay there, I'll lock you in!"

Mary hated Mrs. Medlock for this. "There *was* someone crying, I know there was!" she said to herself. "But I'll discover who it is soon!" She was almost beginning to enjoy herself in Yorkshire.

3

Finding the Secret Garden

When Mary woke up two days later, the wind and rain had all disappeared, and the sky was a beautiful blue.

"Spring'll be here soon," said Martha happily. "You'll love the moor then, when it's full of flowers and birds."

"Could I get to the moor?" asked Mary.

"You've never done much walking, have you? I don't think you could walk the five miles to our cottage!"

"But I'd like to meet your family," Mary said.

Martha looked at the little girl for a moment. She remembered how disagreeable Mary had been when she first arrived. But now, Mary looked interested and friendly.

"I'll ask Mother," said Martha. "She can always think of a good plan. She's sensible, hardworking, and kind—I know you'll like her."

"I like Dickon although I've never seen him."

"I wonder what Dickon will think of you?"

"He won't like me," said Mary. "No one does."

"But do you like yourself? That's what Mother would ask."

"No, not really. I've never thought of that."

"Well, I have to go now. It's my day off, so I'm going home to help Mother with the housework. Goodbye, miss. See you tomorrow."

Mary felt lonelier than ever when Martha had gone, so she went outside. The sunshine made the gardens look different. And the change in the weather had even made Ben Weatherstaff easier to talk to.

"Can you smell spring in the air?" he asked her. "Things are growing, deep down in the ground. Soon you'll see little green shoots coming up—young plants, they are. You watch them."

"Soon you'll see little green shoots coming up."

"I will," replied Mary. "Oh, there's the robin!" The little bird hopped on to Ben's spade. "Are things growing in the garden where he lives?"

"What garden?" said Ben, in his bad-tempered voice.

"You know, the secret garden. Are the flowers dead there?" She really wanted to know the answer.

"Ask the robin," said Ben crossly. "He's the only one who's been in there for the last ten years."

Ten years was a long time, Mary thought. She had been born ten years ago. She walked away, thinking. She had begun to like the gardens, and the robin, and Martha and Dickon and their mother. Before she came to Yorkshire, she had not liked anybody.

She was walking beside the long wall of the secret garden, when a most wonderful thing happened. She suddenly realized the robin was following her. She felt very happy and excited by this and cried out, "You like me, don't you? And I like you too!" As he hopped along beside her, she hopped and sang too, to show him that she was his friend. Just then he stopped at a place where a dog had dug a hole in the ground. As Mary looked at the hole, she noticed something almost buried there. She put her hand in and pulled it out. It was an old key. — Talk loudly

"Perhaps it's been buried for ten years," she whispered to herself. "Perhaps it's the key to the secret garden!"

She looked at it for a long time. How wonderful it would be to find the garden and see what had happened to it in the last ten years! She could play in it all by herself, and nobody would know she was there. She put the key safely in her pocket.

It was an old key.

21

The next morning Martha was back at Misselthwaite Manor and told Mary all about her day with her family.

"I really enjoyed myself. I helped Mother with the whole week's washing and baking. And I told the children about you. They wanted to know about your servants, and the ship that brought you to England, and everything!"

"I can tell you some more for next time," offered Mary. "They'd like to hear about riding on elephants and camels, wouldn't they?"

"Oh, that would be kind of you, miss! And look, Mother has sent you a present!"

*"They'd like to hear about riding on elephants
and camels, wouldn't they?"*

"A present!" repeated Mary. How could a family of fourteen hungry people give anyone a present!

"Mother bought it from a man who came to the door to sell things. She told me, 'Martha, you've brought me your pay, like a good girl, and we need it all, but I'm going to buy something for that lonely child at the Manor,' and she bought one, and here it is!"

It was a jump rope. Mary stared at it.

"What is it?" she asked.

"Don't they have jump ropes in India? Well, this is how you use it. Just watch me."

Martha took the rope and ran into the middle of the room. She counted up to a hundred as she skipped.

"That looks wonderful," said Mary. "Your mother is very kind. Do you think I could ever skip like that?"

"Just try," said Martha. "Mother says it'll make you strong and healthy. Skip outside in the fresh air."

Mary put her coat on and took the jump rope. As she was opening the door, she thought of something and turned around.

"Martha, it was your money really. Thank you." She never thanked people usually, and she did not know how to do it. So she held out her hand because she knew that adults did that.

Martha shook her hand and laughed. "You're a strange child," she said. "Like an old woman! Now run away and play!"

The jump rope was wonderful. Mary counted and

Mary skipped and counted until her face was hot and red.

skipped, skipped and counted, until her face was hot and red. She was having more fun than she had ever had before. She skipped through the gardens until she found Ben Weatherstaff, who was digging and talking to his robin. She wanted them both to see her skip.

"Well!" said Ben. "You're looking fine and healthy today! Go on skipping. It's good for you."

Mary skipped all the way to the secret garden wall. And there was the robin! He had followed her! Mary was very happy.

"You showed me where the key was yesterday," she laughed. "I have it in my pocket. So you ought to show me the door today!"

24

The robin hopped on to an old climbing plant on the wall and sang his most beautiful song. Suddenly the wind made the plant move, and Mary saw something under the dark green leaves. The thick, heavy plant was covering a door. Mary's heart was beating fast, and her hands were shaking as she pushed the leaves away and found the keyhole. She took the key out of her pocket, and it fitted the hole. Using both hands, she managed to unlock the door. Then she turned around to see if anyone was watching. But there was no one, so she pushed the door, which opened, slowly, for the first time in ten years. She walked quickly in and shut the door behind her. At last she was inside the secret garden!

It was the loveliest, most exciting place she had ever seen. There were old rose trees everywhere, and the walls were covered with climbing roses. She looked carefully at the gray branches. Were the roses still alive? Ben would know. She hoped they weren't all dead. But she was *inside* the wonderful garden, in a world of her own. It seemed very strange and silent, but she did not feel lonely at all. Then she noticed some small green shoots coming up through the grass. So something was growing in the garden after all! When she found a lot more shoots in different places, she decided they needed more air and light, so she began to pull out the thick grass around them. She worked away, clearing the ground, for two or three hours, and had to take her coat off because she got so hot. The robin hopped around, happy to see someone gardening.

It was the loveliest, most exciting place Mary had ever seen.

She almost forgot about lunch, and when she arrived back in her room, she was very hungry and ate twice as much as usual. "Martha," she said as she was eating, "I've been thinking. This is a big, lonely house, and there isn't much for me to do. Do you think, if I buy a little spade, I can make my own garden?"

"That's just what Mother said," replied Martha. "You'd enjoy digging and watching plants growing. Dickon can get you a spade and some seeds to plant if you like."

"Oh, thank you, Martha! I have some money that Mrs. Medlock gave me. Will you write and ask Dickon to buy them for me?"

"I will. And he'll bring them to you himself."

"Dickon can get you some seeds to plant."

"Oh! Then I'll see him." Mary looked very excited. Then she remembered something. "I heard that cry in the house again, Martha. It wasn't the wind this time. I've heard it three times now. Who is it?"

Martha looked uncomfortable. "You can't go wandering around the house, you know. Mr. Craven wouldn't like it. Now I have to go and help the others downstairs. I'll see you at tea-time."

As the door closed behind Martha, Mary thought to herself, "This really is the strangest house that anyone ever lived in."

4
Meeting Dickon

Mary spent nearly a week working in the secret garden. Each day she found new shoots coming out of the ground. Soon, there would be flowers everywhere—thousands of them. It was an exciting game to her. When she was inside those beautiful old walls, no one knew where she was.

During that week she became more friendly with Ben, who was often digging in one of the vegetable gardens.

"What are your favorite flowers, Ben?" she asked him one day.

"Roses. I used to work for a young lady who loved roses, you see, and she had a lot in her garden. That was ten years ago. But she died. Very sad, it was."

"What happened to the roses?" asked Mary.

"They were left there, in the garden."

"If rose branches look dry and gray, are they still alive?" asked Mary. It was so important to know!

"In the spring they'll show green shoots, and then—but why are you so interested in roses?" he asked.

Mary's face went red. "I just … wanted to pretend I have a garden. I don't have anyone to play with."

"Well, that's true," said Ben. He seemed to feel sorry for her. Mary decided she liked old Ben, although he was sometimes bad-tempered.

She skipped along and into the wood at the end of the

gardens. Suddenly she heard a strange noise, and there in front of her was a boy. He was sitting under a tree, playing on a wooden pipe. He was about twelve, with a healthy red face and bright blue eyes. There was a squirrel and a crow in the tree, and two rabbits sitting on the grass near him.

There was a squirrel and a crow in the tree, and two rabbits sitting on the grass near him.

"They're listening to the music!" thought Mary. "I shouldn't frighten them!" She stood very still.

The boy stopped playing. "That's right," he said. "Animals don't like it if you move suddenly. I'm Dickon, and you must be Miss Mary. I've brought you the spade and the seeds."

He spoke in an easy, friendly way. Mary liked him at once. As they were looking at the seed packets together, the robin hopped on to a branch near them. Dickon listened carefully to the robin's song.

"He's saying he's your friend," he told Mary.

"Really? Oh, I am happy he likes me. Can you understand everything that birds say?"

"I think I do, and they think I do. I've lived on the moor with them for so long. Sometimes I think I *am* a bird or an animal, not a boy at all!" His smile was the widest she had ever seen.

He explained how to plant the seeds. Suddenly he said, "I can help you plant them! Where's your garden?"

Mary went red, then white. She had never thought of this. What was she going to say?

"Could you keep a secret? It's a great secret. If anyone discovers it, I'll … I'll die!"

"I keep secrets for all the wild birds and animals on the moor. So I can keep yours too," he replied.

"I've stolen a garden," she said very fast. "Nobody goes into it; nobody wants it. I love it, and nobody takes care of it! They're letting it die!" And she threw her arms over her face and started crying.

"Don't cry," said Dickon gently. "Where is it?"

"Come with me, and I'll show you," said Mary.

They went to the secret garden and entered it together. Dickon walked around, looking at everything.

"Martha told me about this place, but I never thought I'd see it," he said. "It's wonderful!"

"What about the roses?" asked Mary worriedly. "Are they still alive? What do you think?"

"Look at these shoots on the branches. Most of them are alive all right." He took out his knife and cut away some of the dead wood from the rose trees. Mary showed him the work she had done in the garden, and they talked as they cut and cleared.

"Dickon," said Mary suddenly, "I like you. I never thought I'd like as many as five people!"

"Only five!" laughed Dickon.

He did look funny when he laughed, thought Mary.

"Yes, your mother, Martha, the robin, Ben, and you." Then she asked him a question in Yorkshire dialect because that was his language.

"Does tha' like me?" was her question.

"Of course! I likes thee wonderful!" replied Dickon, a big smile on his round face. Mary had never been so happy.

When she went back to the house for her lunch, she told Martha about Dickon's visit.

"I have news for you too," said Martha. "Mr. Craven's come home and wants to see you! He's going away again tomorrow, for several months."

"Oh!" said Mary. That was good news. She would have all summer in the secret garden before he came back. But she had to be careful. He couldn't guess her secret now.

Just then Mrs. Medlock arrived, in her best black dress, to take Mary down to Mr. Craven's room.

Mary's uncle had black hair with some white in it, and high, crooked shoulders. His face was not ugly, but very sad. During their conversation he watched her in a worried way. Perhaps he was thinking of other things at the same time.

He looked at the thin child. "Are you well?" he asked. Mary tried to keep her voice calm as she replied,

"I'm getting stronger and healthier."

Mary's uncle had black hair with some white in it,
and high, crooked shoulders.

"What do you want to do, in this big empty house?"

"I … I just want to play outside—I enjoy that."

"Yes, Martha's mother, Susan Sowerby, spoke to me the other day. She's a sensible woman—and she said you needed fresh air. But where do you play?"

"Everywhere! I just skip and run—and look for green shoots. I don't damage anything!"

"Don't look so frightened! Of course a child like you couldn't damage anything. Play where you like. Is there anything that you want?"

Mary came a step nearer to him, and her voice shook a little as she spoke. "Could I—could I have a bit of garden?"

Mr. Craven looked very surprised.

"To plant seeds in … to make them come alive!" Mary went on bravely. "It was too hot in India, so I was always ill and tired there. But here it's different. I … I love the garden!"

He passed a hand quickly over his eyes. Then he looked kindly at Mary. "I knew someone once who loved growing things, like you. Yes, child, take as much of the garden as you want." He smiled gently at her. "Now leave me. I'm very tired."

Mary ran all the way back to her room.

"Martha!" she shouted. "Mr. Craven's really a nice man, but he looks very unhappy. He said I can have my own garden!"

She was planning to work in the garden with Dickon every day, to make it beautiful for the summer.

5
Meeting Colin

I n the middle of the night Mary woke up. Heavy rain had started falling again, and the wind was blowing violently around the walls of the old house. Suddenly she heard crying again. This time she decided to discover who it was. She left her room and in the darkness followed the crying sound, around corners and through doors, up and down stairs, to the other side of the big house. At last she found the right room. She pushed the door open and went in.

It was a big room with beautiful old furniture and pictures. In the large bed was a boy, who looked tired and cross, with a thin, white, tearful face. He stared at Mary.

"Who are you?" he whispered. "Are you a dream?"

"Who are you?" the boy whispered.

"No, I'm not. I'm Mary Lennox. Mr. Craven's my uncle."

"He's my father," said the boy. "I'm Colin Craven."

"No one ever told me he had a son!" said Mary, very surprised.

"Well, no one ever told me you'd come to live here. I'm ill, you see. I don't want people to see me and talk about me. If I live, I may have a crooked back like my father, but I'll probably die."

"What a strange house this is!" said Mary. "So many secrets! Does your father come and see you often?"

"Not often. He doesn't like seeing me because it makes him remember my mother. She died when I was born, so he almost hates me, I think."

"Why do you say you're going to die?" asked Mary.

"I've always been ill. I've nearly died several times, and my back's never been strong. My doctor feels sure that I'm going to die. But he's my father's cousin, and very poor, so he'd like me to die. Then he'd get all the money when my father dies. He gives me medicine and tells me to rest. We had a grand doctor from London once, who told me to go out in the fresh air and try to get well. But I hate fresh air. And another thing, all the servants have to do what I want, because if I'm angry, I become ill."

Mary thought she liked this boy, although he seemed so strange. He asked her lots of questions, and she told him all about her life in India.

"How old are you?" he asked suddenly.

"I'm ten, and so are you," replied Mary, forgetting to be

careful, "because when you were born, the garden door was locked, and the key was buried. And I know that was ten years ago."

Colin sat up in bed and looked very interested. "What door? Who locked it? Where's the key? I want to see it. I'll make the servants tell me where it is. They'll take me there, and you can come too."

"Oh, please! Don't—don't do that!" cried Mary.

Colin stared at her. "Don't you want to see it?"

"Yes, but if you make them open the door, it will never be a secret again. You see, if only *we* know about it, if we—if we can find the key, we can go and play there every day. We can help the garden come alive again. And no one will know about it—except us!"

"I see," said Colin slowly. "Yes, I'd like that. It'll be our secret. I've never had a secret before."

"And perhaps," added Mary cleverly, "we can find a boy to push you in your wheelchair if you can't walk, and we can go there together without any other people. You'll feel better outside. I know I do."

"I'd like that," he said dreamily. "I think I'd like fresh air, in a secret garden."

Then Mary told him about the moor, and Dickon, and Ben Weatherstaff, and the robin, and Colin listened to it all with great interest. He began to smile and look much happier.

"I like having you here," he said. "You have to come and see me every day. But I'm tired now."

"I'll sing you a song. My servant Kamala used to do that in India," said Mary, and very soon Colin was asleep.

The next afternoon Mary visited Colin again, and he seemed very happy to see her. He had sent his nurse away and had told nobody about Mary's visit. Mary had not told anybody either. They read some of his books together and told each other stories. They were enjoying themselves and laughing loudly when suddenly the door opened. Dr. Craven and Mrs. Medlock came in. They almost fell over in surprise.

"What's happening here?" asked Dr. Craven.

Colin sat up straight. To Mary he looked just like an Indian prince. "This is my cousin, Mary Lennox," he said calmly. "I like her. She has to visit me often."

"Oh, I'm sorry, sir," said poor Mrs. Medlock to the

To Mary he looked just like an Indian prince.

37

doctor. "I don't know how she discovered him. I told the servants to keep it a secret."

"Don't be stupid, Medlock," said the Indian prince coldly. "Nobody told her. She heard me crying and found me herself. Bring our tea up now."

"I'm afraid you're getting too hot and excited, my boy," said Dr. Craven. "That's not good for you. Don't forget you're ill."

"I *want* to forget!" said Colin. "I'll be angry if Mary doesn't visit me! She makes me feel better."

Dr. Craven did not look happy when he left the room.

"What a change in the boy, sir!" said the housekeeper. "He's usually so disagreeable with all of us. He really seems to like that strange little girl. And he does look better." Dr. Craven had to agree.

6

Colin Is Afraid

Because it rained all the next week, Mary went to talk to Colin every day instead of visiting the garden. But she woke up early one morning to see the sun shining into her room, and she ran out to the secret garden at once. She did not even wait to have her breakfast. It was beautifully sunny and warm, and a thousand more shoots were pushing their way out of the ground. Dickon was already there, digging hard, with the crow and a young fox beside him.

"Have you seen the robin?" he asked Mary. The little bird was flying busily backwards and forwards as fast as he could, carrying pieces of dry grass.

"He's building a nest!" whispered Mary. They watched the robin for a moment. Then Mary said,

"I have to tell you something. You probably know about Colin Craven, don't you ? Well, I've met him, and I'm going to help him to get better."

"He's building a nest!" whispered Mary.

39

"That's good news." There was a big smile on Dickon's honest face. "We all knew he was ill."

"He's afraid he'll have a crooked back like his father. I think that's what's making him ill."

"Perhaps we can bring him here and let him rest under the trees. That'll do him good. That's what we'll do."

They had a lot of gardening and planning to do, and Mary did not have time to visit Colin that day. When she came back to the house in the evening, Martha told her that the servants had had trouble with Colin.

"He's been very bad-tempered all afternoon with all of us because you didn't come, miss."

"Well, I was busy. He'll have to learn not to be so selfish," replied Mary coldly. She forgot how selfish *she* had been when she was ill in India. "I'll go and see him now."

When she went into his room, he was lying in bed, looking tired. He did not turn to look at her.

"What's the matter with you?" she asked crossly.

"My back aches, and my head hurts. Why didn't you come this afternoon?"

"I was working in the garden with Dickon."

"I won't let that boy come to the garden if you stay with him instead of talking to me!"

Mary suddenly became very angry. "If you send Dickon away, I'll never come into this room again!"

"You'll have to if I say so. I'll make the servants bring you in here."

"Oh, will you, prince! But no one can make me talk to

you. I won't look at you. I'll stare at the floor!"

"You selfish girl!" cried Colin.

"You're more selfish than I am. You're the most selfish boy I've ever met!"

"I'm not as selfish as your fine Dickon! He keeps you playing outside when he knows I'm ill and alone!"

Mary had never been so furious. "Dickon is nicer than any other boy in the world! He's like an angel!"

"An angel! Don't make me laugh! He's just a poor country boy, with holes in his shoes!"

"He's a thousand times better than you are!"

Colin had never argued with anyone like himself in his life, and in fact it was good for him. But now he was beginning to feel sorry for himself.

"I'm always ill," he said, and he started to cry. "I'm sure my back is a bit crooked. And I'm going to die!"

"No, you're not!" said Mary crossly.

Colin opened his eyes very wide. Nobody had said that to him before. He was angry, but a bit happy at the same time. "What do you mean? You know I'm going to die! Everybody says I'm going to die!"

"I don't believe it!" said Mary in her most disagreeable voice. "You just say that to make people feel sorry for you. You're too horrid to die!"

Colin forgot about his painful back and sat up in bed. "Get out of the room at once!" he shouted, and he threw a book at her.

"I'm going," Mary shouted in reply, "and I won't come

"Get out of the room at once!" Colin shouted.

back!" The door banged shut behind her.

When she reached her own room, she had decided never to tell him her great secret. "He can stay in his room and die if he wants!" she thought. But soon she began to remember how ill he had been, and how frightened he was, frightened that one day his back would become as crooked as his father's. "Perhaps … perhaps I'll go back and see him tomorrow!"

That night she was woken by the most terrible screams that she had ever heard. Servants were opening and shutting doors and running about.

"It's Colin!" thought Mary. "He'll go on screaming until he makes himself really ill! How selfish he is! Somebody should stop him!"

Just then Martha ran into the room. "We don't know what to do!" she cried. "He likes you, miss! Come and see if you can make him calmer, please!"

"Well, I'm very cross with him," said Mary, and jumped out of bed. "I'm going to stop him!"

"That's right," said Martha. "He needs someone like you to argue with. It'll give him something new to think about."

Mary ran into Colin's room, right up to his bed.

"Stop screaming!" she shouted furiously. "Stop at once! I hate you! Everybody hates you! You'll die if you go on screaming like this, and I hope you will!"

The screams stopped immediately. This was the first time that anyone had spoken so angrily to Colin, and he was shocked. But he went on crying quietly to himself.

"My back's becoming crooked, I can feel it! I know I'm going to die!" Large tears ran down his face.

"Don't be stupid!" cried Mary. "There's nothing the matter with your horrid back! Martha, come here and help me look at his back!"

Martha and Mrs. Medlock were standing at the door, staring at Mary, their mouths half open. They both looked very frightened. Martha came forward to help, and Miss Mary looked carefully at Colin's thin white back, up and down. Her face was serious and angry at the same time. The room was very quiet.

"There's nothing wrong with your back!" Mary said at last.

"There's nothing wrong with your back!" she said at last. "Nothing at all! It's as straight as mine!"

Only Colin knew how important those crossly spoken, childish words were. All his life he had been afraid to ask about his back, and his terrible fear had made him ill. Now an angry little girl told him his back was straight, and he believed her. He was no longer afraid.

They were both calmer now. He gave Mary his hand. "I think—I'm almost sure I will live if we can go out in the garden together sometimes. I'm very tired now. Will you stay with me until I go to sleep?"

The servants went out very quietly.

"I'll tell you all about the secret garden," whispered Mary. "I think it's full of roses and beautiful flowers. Birds like making their nests there because it's so quiet and safe. And perhaps our robin ..."

But Colin was already asleep.

The next day Mary met Dickon as usual in the secret garden and told him about Colin. Mary loved Dickon's Yorkshire dialect and was trying to learn it herself. She spoke a little now.

"We mun get poor Colin out here in th' sunshine—an' we munnot lose no time about it!"

Dickon laughed. "Well done! I didn't know you could speak Yorkshire! You're right. We need to bring Colin to the garden as soon as we can."

So that afternoon she went to see Colin.

"I'm sorry I said I'd send Dickon away," he said. "I hated you when you said he was like an angel!"

"Well, he's a funny kind of angel, but he understands wild animals better than anyone." Suddenly, Mary knew that this was the right moment to tell him. She caught hold of his hands. "Colin, this is important. Can you keep a secret?"

"Yes—yes!" he whispered excitedly. "What is it?"

"We've found the door into the secret garden!"

"Oh Mary! Will I live long enough to see it?"

"Of course you will! Don't be stupid!" said Mary crossly. But it was a very natural thing to say, and they both laughed.

Colin told Mrs. Medlock and the doctor that he wanted to go out in his wheelchair. At first the doctor was worried the boy would get too tired, but when he heard that Dickon would push the wheelchair, he agreed.

"Dickon's a sensible boy," he told Colin. "But don't forget—"

"I've told you, I *want* to forget that I'm ill," said Colin in his prince's voice. "Don't you understand ? It's because my cousin makes me forget that I feel better when I'm with her."

7
Colin and the Garden

Of course, it was most important that no one should see Colin, Mary, or Dickon entering the secret garden. So Colin gave orders to the gardeners that they all had to keep away from that part of the garden in future.

The next afternoon Colin was carried downstairs by a man servant and put in his wheelchair outside the front door. Dickon arrived, with his crow, two squirrels, and the fox, and started pushing the wheelchair gently away from the house and into the gardens. Mary walked beside the chair.

Spring had really arrived now, and it seemed very exciting to Colin, who had lived indoors for so long. He smelled the warm air from the moor and watched the little white clouds in the blue sky. In a very short time he heard Mary say, "This is where I found the key ... and this is the door ... and this ... this is the secret garden!"

Colin covered his eyes with his hands until he was inside the four high walls and the door was shut again. Then he looked around at the roses climbing the old red walls, the pink and white flowers on the fruit trees, and the birds and the butterflies everywhere. The sun warmed his face, and he suddenly knew he felt different.

"Mary! Dickon!" he cried. "I'm going to get better! I'm going to live for ever and ever and ever!"

As Dickon pushed the wheelchair all around the garden,

he told Colin the names of all the plants. The sun shone, the birds sang, and in every corner of the garden there was something interesting to look at. The three children talked and laughed, and by the end of the afternoon all three were speaking Yorkshire together.

"I'll come back here every afternoon," said Colin. "I want to watch things growing."

"Soon you'll be strong enough to walk and dig. You'll

Dickon pushed the wheelchair all around the garden.

be able to help us with the gardening," said Dickon kindly.

"Do you really think I'll be able to … to walk and … dig?" asked Colin.

"Of course you will. You have legs, like us!"

"But they're not very strong," answered Colin. "They shake, and … and I'm afraid to stand on them."

"When you want to use them, you'll be able to," said Dickon. The garden was quiet for a moment.

Suddenly Colin said, "Who's that?" Mary turned her head and noticed Ben Weatherstaff's angry face looking at her over the garden wall.

"What are you doing in that garden, young miss?" he shouted. He had not seen Colin or Dickon.

"The robin showed me the way, Ben," she replied.

"You … you—" He stopped shouting, and his mouth dropped open as he saw Dickon pushing a boy in a wheelchair over the grass towards him.

"Do you know who I am?" asked the boy in the chair.

Old Ben stared. "You have your mother's eyes," he said in a shaking voice. "Yes, I know you. You're Mr. Craven's son, the little boy with the crooked back."

Colin forgot that he had ever had backache. "My back's as straight as yours is!" he shouted.

Ben stared and stared. He only knew what he had heard from the servants. "You don't have a crooked back?" he asked. "Or crooked legs?"

That was too much. Colin was furious, and it made him feel strong.

"Come here, Dickon!" he shouted, and threw off his blanket. Dickon was by his side in a second. Mary felt sick with fear. Could Colin stand?

Then Colin's thin feet were on the grass, and he was standing, holding Dickon's arm. He looked strangely tall, and he held his head very high.

"Look at me!" he shouted at Ben. "Just look at me!"

"He's as straight as any boy in Yorkshire!" said Dickon.

Tears were running down Ben's brown old face. "They said you were going to die!" he whispered.

"Well, you can see that's not true," said Colin. "Now, get down from the wall and come here. I want to talk to you. You've got to help us keep the garden a secret."

"Yes, sir," said old Ben, as he dried his eyes.

"Look at me!" Colin shouted at Ben. "Just look at me!"

That was the first of many beautiful afternoons in the secret garden. Colin was brought there by Dickon and Mary nearly every day, and he saw all the changes that happened there during the spring and early summer. Ben Weatherstaff, now in on the secret, joined them as often as he could.

One day Colin spoke to all of them. "Listen, everybody. I think there's something like magic that makes gardens grow and things happen. Perhaps if I believe in it, the magic will make me strong. Let's all sit down in a circle and ask the magic to work."

So they all sat on the grass in a circle, Dickon with his crow, his fox, and the two squirrels, Mary, Colin, and Ben. Colin repeated these words several times. "The sun's shining. That's the magic. Being strong. That's the magic. Magic! Help me! Magic! Help me!"

At last Colin stopped. "Now I'm going to walk around the garden," he said, and took Dickon's arm. Slowly he walked from one wall to another, followed closely by Mary and Ben. And when he had walked all the way around, he said, "You see! I can walk now! The magic worked!"

"It's wonderful!" cried Mary. "Your father will think he is dreaming when he sees you!"

"I won't tell him yet. I'm going to keep it a secret from everybody. I'll come to the garden and walk and run a little more every day until I'm as healthy as any other boy. Then, when my father comes home, I'll walk up to him and say, 'Here I am, Father. You see? I'm not going to die!' "

Now began a difficult time for Colin and Mary. Dickon told his mother about it one evening as he was digging the cottage garden.

"You see, mother, they don't want the doctor or the servants to guess that Colin can walk and is getting better. So they have to pretend he's still ill and just as disagreeable as he used to be!"

"If they're running about all day in the fresh air, that'll make them hungry, I should think!"

"Yes, that's the problem. They're both getting fatter and healthier, and they really enjoy their food now. But they have to send some of it back to the kitchen, uneaten. If they eat it all, people will realize how healthy they are! Sometimes they're very hungry!"

"I know what we can do," said Mrs. Sowerby. "You can take some fresh milk and some of my newly baked bread to the garden in the mornings. If they have that, it'll do them a lot of good! What a game those children are playing!" And she laughed until tears came to her eyes.

One afternoon when they were all working in the garden, the door opened, and a woman came quietly in.

"It's Mother!" cried Dickon, and ran towards her. "I told her where the

"It's Mother!"

door was because I knew she would keep the secret."

Colin held out his hand to her. "I've wanted to see you for a long time," he said.

"Dear boy!" Susan Sowerby whispered, holding his hand. "You're so like your mother!"

"Do you think," asked Colin carefully, "that will make my father like me?"

"I'm sure it will," she answered warmly. "He has to see you—he has to come home now."

"You see how healthy the boy is, Susan?" asked old Ben. "Look how strong and straight his legs are now!"

"Yes," she laughed. "Playing and working outside, and eating good Yorkshire food, has made him strong. And Miss Mary too," she added, turning to Mary. "Mrs. Medlock heard that your mother was a pretty woman. You'll soon be as pretty as she was."

"Do you believe in magic?" Colin asked her.

"I do," she answered, "but everybody gives it a different name. It makes the sun shine and the seeds grow—and it has made you healthy."

She sat down on the grass and stayed for a while, talking and laughing with the children in the quiet, sunny garden. When she stood up to leave, Colin suddenly put out a hand to her.

"I wish—you were my mother!" he whispered.

Mrs. Sowerby put her arms around him and held him to her. "Dear boy! You're as close to your mother as you could be, here in her garden. And your father'll come back soon!"

8
Mr. Craven Comes Home

While the secret garden was returning to life, a man with high, crooked shoulders was wandering around the most beautiful places in Europe. For ten years he had lived this lonely life, his heart full of sadness and his head full of dark dreams. Everywhere he went, he carried his unhappiness with him like a black cloud. Other travelers thought he was half mad or a man who could not forget some terrible crime. His name was Archibald Craven.

But one day, as he sat by a mountain stream, he actually looked at a flower, and for the first time in ten years he realized how beautiful something living could be. The valley seemed very quiet as he sat there, staring at the flower. He felt strangely calm.

But one day, as he sat by a mountain stream,
he actually looked at a flower.

"What is happening to me?" he whispered. "I feel different—I almost feel I'm alive again!"

At that moment, hundreds of miles away in Yorkshire, Colin was seeing the secret garden for the first time, and saying, "I'm going to live for ever and ever and ever!" But Mr. Craven did not know this.

That night, in his hotel room, he slept better than usual. As the weeks passed, he even began to think a little about his home and his son. One evening in late summer, as he was sitting quietly beside a lake, he felt the strange calmness again. He fell asleep and had a dream that seemed very real. He heard a voice calling him. It was sweet and clear and happy, the voice of his young wife.

"Archie! Archie! Archie!"

"My dear!" He jumped up. "Where are you?"

"In the garden!" called the beautiful voice.

And then the dream ended. In the morning, when he woke up, he remembered the dream.

"She says she's in the garden!" he thought. "But the door's locked, and the key's buried."

That morning he received a letter from Susan Sowerby. In it she asked him to come home, but she did not give a reason. Mr. Craven thought of his dream and decided to return to England immediately. On the long journey back to Yorkshire, he was thinking about Colin.

"I wonder how he is! I wanted to forget him because he makes me think of his mother. He lived, and she died! But perhaps I've been wrong. Susan Sowerby says I should go home, so perhaps she thinks I can help him."

When he arrived home, he found the housekeeper very confused about Colin's health.

"He's very strange, sir," said Mrs. Medlock. "He looks better, it's true, but some days he eats nothing at all, and other days he eats just like a healthy boy. He used to scream even at the idea of fresh air, but now he spends all his time outside in his wheelchair, with Miss Mary and Dickon Sowerby. He's in the garden at the moment."

"In the garden!" repeated Mr. Craven. Those were the words of the dream! He hurried out of the house and towards the place which he had not visited for so long. He found the door with the climbing plant over it and stood outside, listening, for a moment.

"Surely I can hear voices inside the garden?" he thought. "Aren't there children whispering, laughing, and running in there? Or am I going mad?"

And then the moment came when the children could not stay quiet. There was wild laughing and shouting, and the door was thrown open. A boy ran out, a tall, healthy, handsome boy, straight into the man's arms. Mr. Craven stared into the boy's laughing eyes.

"Who—What? Who?" he cried.

Colin had not planned to meet his father like this. But perhaps this was the best way, to come running out with his cousin and his friend.

"Father," he said, "I'm Colin. You can't believe it! I can't believe it myself. It was the garden, and Mary and Dickon

A boy ran out, a tall, healthy, handsome boy,
straight into the man's arms.

and the magic, that made me well. We've kept it a secret up to now. Aren't you happy, Father? I'm going to live for ever and ever and ever!"

Mr. Craven put his hands on the boy's shoulders. For a moment he could not speak. "Take me into the garden, my boy," he said at last, "and tell me all about it."

And in the secret garden, where the roses were at their best and the butterflies were flying from flower to flower in the summer sunshine, they told Colin's father their story. Sometimes he laughed, and sometimes he cried, but most of the time he just looked, unbelieving, into the handsome face of the son that he had almost forgotten.

"Now," said Colin at the end, "it isn't a secret any more. I'll never use the wheelchair again. I'm going to walk back with you, Father—to the house."

And so, that afternoon, Mrs. Medlock, Martha, and the other servants had the greatest shock of their lives. Through the gardens towards the house came Mr. Craven, looking happier than they had ever seen him. And by his side, with his shoulders straight, his head held high, and a smile on his lips, walked young Colin!

GLOSSARY

angel a messenger from God, or a very good person

bad-tempered often cross and angry

bury (past tense **buried**) to put a person or thing in the ground

confused not able to think clearly, or to understand something

cousin the child of your uncle or aunt

dialect a different way of speaking the same language in a different part of the country (e.g., Yorkshire)

disagreeable not pleasing; bad-tempered

furious very angry

handsome good-looking (usually for a boy or man)

hop (past tense **hopped**) to jump on one foot

horrid bad, terrible, not at all nice

magic something strange that can make wonderful, unusual things happen

shocked very surprised (by something unpleasant)

skip (past tense **skipped**) to jump again and again over a rope that you are swinging

stare to look at someone or something for a long time

tears drops of water that come from your eyes when you cry

ugly not beautiful

wander to walk slowly with no special plan

whisper to speak very softly and quietly

YORKSHIRE DIALECT
USED IN THIS STORY

Tha' canna' dress thysen?

You can't dress yourself?

Does tha' like me?

Do you like me?

I likes thee wonderful.

I like you wonderfully.

We mun get poor Colin out here in th' sunshine, an' we munnot lose no time about it.

We have to get poor Colin out here in the sunshine, and we can't lose any time about it.

Before Reading

1 **Read the story introduction on the first page of the book and the back cover. What do you know now about Mary Lennox? For each sentence, circle Y (Yes) or N (No).**

1 She is from India. Y/N
2 She moves to a large house in Yorkshire. Y/N
3 She has a lot of friends. Y/N
4 Both she and Ben Weatherstaff are bad-tempered. Y/N
5 She often cries in the night. Y/N

2 **Why is the garden locked? Choose one of these ideas.**

The secret garden is locked because . . .
1 nobody wants to use it.   4 a murder happened there.
2 somebody died there.   5 there is a dangerous animal
3 a ghost was seen there.   inside it.

3 **What is going to happen in this story? Can you guess the answers to these questions?**

1 How can Mary find a way into the garden?
2 Will she make some friends?
3 Will Ben help her or make life more difficult for her?
4 How will her uncle feel about her?
5 Will Mary change during the story or stay the same?

ACTIVITIES

While Reading

Read Chapter 1. Who said this, and to whom? What, or who, were they talking about?

1 "I'll hit her when she comes back!" *Mary, To Kamala*
2 "People are dying like flies." *Young Englishman - To mary Mother*
3 "It's the child, the one nobody ever saw!" *Mary, To Two Man*
4 "He has a crooked back, and he's horrid!" *Basil, To Mary*
5 "You have to stay out of his way."
6 "I don't like it."

Read Chapter 2, and answer these questions.

Who . . .   *Martha*
1 . . . was going to clean Mary's room and bring her food?
2 . . . sometimes rode a wild horse on the moor? *Dickon*
3 . . . told Mary that the secret garden was not her business?
4 . . . hated the secret garden, and why?
5 . . . told Mary to stay in her room and not wander around the house? *Mrs Medlock*

Before you read Chapter 3 (*Finding the Secret Garden*), can you guess what is going to happen?

1 Will Mary find the buried key, and if so, how?
2 Who will show her where the secret garden is?
3 What will she find inside the garden?

Read Chapter 3. Choose the best question-word for these questions, and then answer them.

What / Who / Why

1 What did Martha do on her day off?
2 Who showed Mary where the key was buried?
3 What did Mrs. Sowerby buy for Mary?
4 What did Mary do when she got inside the secret garden?
5 Why did Mary want a little spade?
6 What had Mary now heard three times in the house?

Read Chapter 4. Are these sentences true (T) or false (F)? Rewrite the false sentences with the correct information.

T 1 Ben used to work in a garden which had a lot of roses. T
F 2 Dickon brought a wild horse when he came to see Mary. F
F 3 Mary did not tell anybody about the secret garden. T
T 4 Mr. Craven told Mary she could have her own garden. F
T 5 Mary thought that her uncle was a horrid man. T

Read Chapters 5 and 6, and answer these questions.

1 How did Mary find Colin? She followed the crying
2 Why didn't Mr. Craven visit his son very often? what is gaso~
3 What was the matter with Colin? felling good
4 Why was the robin so busy in the garden?
5 What was Mary's plan for Colin?
6 Why was the argument good for Colin's health?
7 Why did Mary look at Colin's back?
8 How was Colin going to get to the secret garden?

62

Before you read Chapters 7 and 8 (the titles are *Colin and the Garden* and *Mr. Craven Comes Home*), can you guess what happens? Choose Y (Yes) or N (No) for each of these ideas.

1 Colin gets well and learns to walk again. Y/N
2 The children tell everybody their secret. Y/N
3 Colin dies in the garden. Y/N
4 Mr. Craven is angry, and locks the garden up again. Y/N

Read Chapters 7 and 8. Match these halves of sentences and join them with the linking words. (Use each word once.)

and / because / so / until / when / which / while

A

1 _When_ Colin first saw the beautiful secret garden, 12
2 He wanted to show Ben that he did not have crooked legs, 8
3 After that, he walked and ran a little more each day, 11
4 _While_ the secret garden and Colin were returning to life, 14
5 In late summer he decided to return to Yorkshire, 9
6 He came to the door of the garden 13
7 Then the children told him all about the magic of the secret garden, 10

B

8 _So_ he got out of his wheelchair and stood up straight.
9 _because_ in a dream he heard his dead wife calling to him.
10 _which_ had made Colin well.
11 _Until_ he was as strong and healthy as any other boy.
12 he knew at once that he was going to get better.
13 _and_ his son ran out, straight into his arms.
14 Mr. Craven was traveling around Europe.

After Reading

1 **Choose suitable adjectives to complete these sentences about people in the story. (You can use some adjectives twice.)**

bad-tempered, beautiful, crooked, disagreeable, fresh, friendly, frightened, gentle, good, healthy, ill, interested, kind, lonely, new, sad, selfish, shocked, sorry, strong, wild

1 When Mary arrived in Yorkshire, she was _____ because she had no friends. She only thought of herself and was _____ and _____. But playing outside in the _____ air soon made her _____ and _____, and she became more _____ in other people.

2 Martha was always _____ and _____ to Mary, but she was _____ when she learned that Mary couldn't dress herself.

3 Before he met Mary, Colin was always feeling _____ for himself. He was _____ that his back would be _____ like his father's, and this fear had made him _____. Meeting Mary was _____ for him and gave him _____ things to think about.

4 Old Ben Weatherstaff was often _____ with Mary, but his voice was always _____ when he spoke to the robin.

5 Dickon was a _____ boy, who could make friends with _____ animals.

6 Mr. Craven spent his time traveling in _____ places, but he was a _____ and _____ man.

2 **When Martha went home on her day off, she told her mother all about the little girl who had just arrived from India. Complete Mrs. Sowerby's part of the conversation.**

MARTHA: Did you know, Mother, there's a little girl who's come to live at the Manor? Her name's Mary Lennox.

MRS. SOWERBY: _____

MARTHA: From India. Her parents both died suddenly, so she had to come to live with Mr. Craven, her uncle.

MRS. SOWERBY: _____

MARTHA: She's a very strange little girl. Very thin, with a yellow skin. And she doesn't know how to dress herself because her servant always used to do it for her.

MRS. SOWERBY: _____

MARTHA: Oh yes, I told her that.

MRS. SOWERBY: _____

MARTHA: I feel sorry for her too. And you're right, she *is* lonely. I talk to her a lot when I take her meals up.

MRS. SOWERBY: _____

MARTHA: Well, I told her all about the locked garden and why nobody's been in it for ten years.

MRS. SOWERBY: _____

MARTHA: No, I didn't. Mrs. Medlock told all the servants that we shouldn't say anything about him.

MRS. SOWERBY: _____

MARTHA: Yes, I'm afraid she will. She's already heard him crying and asked me about it.

MRS. SOWERBY: _____

MARTHA: A jump rope? Oh yes, that's a wonderful idea!

3 In this word search there is a hidden sentence about the story. Can you find it? Use these clues to help you.

CLUES

1 The letters in each word go from left to right or from top to bottom.
2 The first and the fourth words in the sentence are only one letter long.
3 Words follow each other. At the end of a word, look for the beginning of the next word in the same square, the square above, below, or to the right.
4 There are twelve words in the sentence.
5 The sentence begins in the top left box.

There are another twelve words in the word search, which do not belong to the sentence. What are they?

A	B	F	N	O	K	M	A	G	I	C	Q	E	H	O	P
P	O	V	G	I	R	L	Z	E	B	D	O	O	R	K	A
C	Y	J	A	H	I	E	N	H	O	L	R	B	H	E	H
O	A	N	D	R	X	A	E	M	S	P	A	D	E	Y	G
U	D	B	H	O	C	R	G	T	U	I	C	X	T	H	E
S	M	O	E	B	M	N	O	C	F	H	J	I	N	L	G
I	W	Q	A	I	P	E	L	H	A	P	P	Y	S	N	A
N	N	E	L	N	V	D	B	E	K	T	O	V	K	U	R
R	E	B	T	R	E	T	O	I	P	N	S	I	I	Y	D
B	S	G	H	A	C	J	H	O	R	R	I	D	P	F	E
U	T	I	Y	S	E	E	D	V	A	O	M	B	I	H	N

66

4 Perhaps this is what some of the people in the story were thinking. Who are they, and who were they thinking about? What was happening in the story at the time?

1 "Was it a dream? No, I'm sure it wasn't. I really do have a cousin. She said she'd come and see me today, but I'm not going to tell anybody about her. I *like* having secrets . . . "

2 "He has to come home soon. I'm sure it will change his life, to see his boy so well and happy. I'm going to go home now and write a letter to him at once . . . "

3 "Where am I? Oh yes, I remember now. But who's that, cleaning the fireplace? Oh, it's only a servant. I suppose she's going to be *my* servant. I'll ask her . . . "

4 "The boy's no more crooked than I am. And those eyes— just like his mother's! But he wants to talk to me. I have to get down from the wall and go and find the door . . . "

5 "I know my secret's safe with him. He thought the garden was wonderful—and he knows all about roses and seeds. I really like him. And he said he liked me, too!"

5 Do you agree (A) or disagree (D) with these sentences about the people in the story? Explain why.

1 Mary was a disagreeable child because her parents did not love her or take care of her.
2 Mr. Craven was a bad father to Colin.
3 Colin was a more selfish person than Mary.
4 Dickon was a better friend for Mary than Colin was.

ABOUT THE AUTHOR

Frances Eliza Hodgson Burnett was born in Manchester, England, in 1849. When she was sixteen, her family went to the USA and made their home in Knoxville, Tennessee. There, she began to write stories for magazines, and after marrying in 1873, she went on writing stories for both adults and children. *Little Lord Fauntleroy*, in 1886, made her famous, and in 1905 came another famous book, *A Little Princess* (retold in the Oxford Bookworms Library, at Stage 1), which has been filmed several times. *The Secret Garden* came out in 1910. By this time Burnett had two homes—a house in Kent, in the south of England, and a house on Long Island in the USA, where she died in 1924.

Both *Little Lord Fauntleroy* and *A Little Princess* are about nice, good children. Many parents bought these books, hoping that their own children would learn from the little lord and the "little princess" how to be good. Today, most people think *The Secret Garden* is Burnett's best book. In this story the children are more like real children—they are selfish and disagreeable, they shout and get angry, they learn and they change.

The idea for the book came to Burnett from the old rose garden at her home in Kent, where she made friends, like Mary in the story, with a robin that came to take bread from her hand. The story is still a great favorite with children, who love the idea of a secret place that adults do not know about. The most recent film of the book was made in 1993—one of many films of this famous and much-loved story.

OXFORD BOOKWORMS LIBRARY

Classics • Crime & Mystery • Factfiles • Fantasy & Horror
Human Interest • Playscripts • Thriller & Adventure
True Stories • World Stories

The OXFORD BOOKWORMS LIBRARY provides enjoyable reading in English, with a wide range of classic and modern fiction, non-fiction, and plays. It includes original and adapted texts in seven carefully graded language stages which take learners from beginner to advanced level.

All Stage 1 titles, as well as over eighty other titles from Starter to Stage 6, are available as audio recordings. All Starters and many titles at Stages 1 to 4 are specially recommended for younger learners. Every Bookworm is illustrated, and Starters and Factfiles have full-color illustrations.

The OXFORD BOOKWORMS LIBRARY also offers extensive support. Each book contains an introduction to the story, notes about the author, a glossary, and activities. Additional resources include tests and worksheets, as well as answers for these and for the activities in the books. There is advice on running a class library, using audio recordings, and the many ways of using Oxford Bookworms in reading programs. Resource materials are available on the website <www.oup.com/bookworms>.

The *Oxford Bookworms Collection* is a series for advanced learners. It consists of volumes of short stories by well-known authors, both classic and modern. Texts are not abridged or adapted in any way, but carefully selected to be accessible to the advanced student.

You can find details and a full list of titles in the *Oxford Bookworms Library Catalog* and *Oxford English Language Teaching Catalogs*, and on the website <www.oup.com/bookworms>.

A Christmas Carol

CHARLES DICKENS

Retold by Clare West

Christmas is humbug, Scrooge says—just a time when you find yourself a year older and not a penny richer. The only thing that matters to Scrooge is business, and making money.

But on Christmas Eve three spirits come to visit him. They take him traveling on the wings of the night to see the shadows of Christmas past, present, and future—and Scrooge learns a lesson that he will never forget.

Frankenstein

MARY SHELLEY

Retold by Patrick Nobes

Victor Frankenstein thinks he has found the secret of life. He takes parts from dead people and builds a new "man." But this monster is so big and frightening that everyone runs away from him—even Frankenstein himself!

The monster is like an enormous baby who needs love. But nobody gives him love, and soon he learns to hate. And, because he is so strong, the next thing he learns is how to kill …

The Call of the Wild

JACK LONDON

Retold by Nick Bullard

When men find gold in the frozen north of Canada, they need dogs—big, strong dogs to pull the sleds on the long journeys to and from the gold mines.

Buck is stolen from his home in the south and sold as a sled-dog. He has to learn a new way of life—how to work in harness, how to stay alive in the ice and the snow ... and how to fight. Because when a dog falls down in a fight, he never gets up again.

BOOKWORMS · FANTASY & HORROR · STAGE 4

Dr. Jekyll and Mr. Hyde

ROBERT LOUIS STEVENSON

Retold by Rosemary Border

You are walking through the streets of London. It is getting dark, and you want to get home quickly. You enter a narrow side-street. Everything is quiet, but as you pass the door of a large windowless building, you hear a key turning in the lock. A man comes out and looks at you. You have never seen him before, but you realize immediately that he hates you. You are shocked to discover, also, that you hate him.

Who is this man that everybody hates? And why is he coming out of the laboratory of the very respectable Dr. Jekyll?

A Tale of Two Cities

CHARLES DICKENS

Retold by Ralph Mowat

"The Marquis lay there, like stone, with a knife pushed into his heart. On his chest lay a piece of paper, with the words: *Drive him fast to the grave. This is from JACQUES.*"

The French Revolution brings terror and death to many people. But even in these troubled times people can still love and be kind. They can be generous, true-hearted ... and brave.

Little Women

LOUISA MAY ALCOTT

Retold by John Escott

When Christmas comes for the four March girls, there is no money for expensive presents, and they give away their Christmas breakfast to a poor family. But there are no happier girls in America than Meg, Jo, Beth, and Amy. They miss their father, of course, who is away at the Civil War, but they try hard to be good so that he will be proud of his "little women" when he comes home.

This heart-warming story of family life has been popular for more than a hundred years.